Permanence is Temporary

Sierra (C.J.) Morris

BookLeaf Publishing

India | USA | UK

Presentation by *BookLeaf Publishing*

Web: www.bookleafpub.com

E-mail: info@bookleafpub.com

ISBN: 9789363302686

First edition 2024

To: Those in the Process of Staying, Letting
Go, or Becoming.

ACKNOWLEDGEMENT

Thank you to every person I've met, interacted with, and contributed to my life in some way.

My past friends, my current friends, and my future friends.

PREFACE

A small preface, a poem - 'Something Like Poetry.'

The quietest voice has the loudest mind.
Why is this, what we've come to find?
We design and refine our identity around what seems to align with confined views of this world, what is and what has been.
We're inclined to try our best to fit in.
So those whose thoughts are louder than words,
We tend to hold them inside, until they rot and crumble, turn stale and cold.
Or until they become something- anything- worth admiring and attempting to understand, hold onto, and let drip through your fingers, feeling the reality, the weight of a thought- something brave and brilliant and bold.
It's not that my head is a vacant space, it's not that I'm nervous of judgment or fear.
Knots with tangled galaxies lie dormant in my brain,
If you know me by more than just my name, you'll understand what I mean.
I can talk for hours, for days, and write novels with the voices in my head as the authors.

It's not that I'm distracted, I notice everything-
to the point where it becomes overwhelming.
String, connected by the tiniest of pins, forming
a mess with no beginning or end- how do you
express feelings like that in mere, ordinary
classroom words?
That's why I'm here.
I have a voice that doesn't fit in my body, so
where else can it fit but inside the deepest
crevices inside the pages of a poem?
Doodles in the margins of my math homework,
tear-stained hoodie sleeves, and essays that are
five pages too long.
I remain secluded and silent because if I were to
open my mouth, and unapologetically let my
brain spill, it would never close until I manage
to express every thought a single
human can have in their finite existence, or until
my heart finally ceases its rhythm.
Whichever comes first.

Poems, for me, are a way to drain those ideas, let
them flow into a tangible product, limited in
vocabulary without rambling for hours- I can
share. I'd love to share.
I won't change the world with poems. But
hopefully, I can add to it.
Hopefully, I can change the world in other ways.

I am here in life. I'm making differences in the smallest ways.

And I hope someday I can make someone feel as deeply as I do through my words, and inspire them to translate those deep, profound, and monstrous feelings into-

Something that could help people, change the world, change our views, and give each person a voice, finally.

Something like a way to translate those wonderful views of processing our world into a finite, deconstructible piece of art.

Something like poetry.

Let Me Make My Mark

Who has time for creativity these days?
Draining, the days are, as they fray away.
Like the fabric of my favorite shirt,
It hurts.
How fast the days pass, my energy the last thing
to catch up,
By the time I have time, I'm down to my last
dime as my spirit fades.
And all of the inspiration my brain gathered
from the morning, I mourn,
As it buries itself in the forgotten graveyard of
my memories and ideas that were never made.
Delayed, was my creativity, so decayed are those
thoughts.
What could have been, will never be.
Because I'm too damn tired to write my
thoughts freely.
To some degree, it brings such a sting,
Grating, are the mornings.
Repetitive, endless mornings, with my emotions
stirring-
Stewing, sitting-
Like a bubbling cauldron waiting for the last
ingredient.

But I'm bent out of shape, my brain is dented,
my eyes are sagging, as these days keep
dragging-
Is it too much to ask to create?
This terrible state of hating my fate, being
destined to barely invent.
They ask how I am and they expect a sentence,
this messed up dance, I'm in a trance, waiting for
something to snap me out of it.
When someone asks if I'm ok, why can't I
respond in a drawing? A poem?
They expect paragraphs, I want to write stanzas.
Lines and verses, so they know what I stand as.
I have so much inside, and too little time or
energy to write it.
The act of creating is gorgeous and draining.
I'm a bomb waiting to explode, a pipe
overflowing,
Please just let me flow- let me go- let me show
you what I can make with my own mind and two
hands when I truly can think with this time I've
been given- I'm already seventeen please just let
me stop, and change the world with what I can
do, I promise it's more than it seems.
But- I can't.
The faucet of my creative flow turns off with a
sudden squeak.
As it drip… drip…. Drips…..

Into the doodles on my math homework. Three line poems in the corner of my notebooks. When I shade in the letters of a worksheet. When I color code my notes in class. When I design my slideshows to match with the subject so seamlessly-
I hate how that's all I can do, in this confined space and time.
I can be so much more- this is the smallest, terrible taste- the crust of my creative potential please just let me thrive.
What doesn't thrive, goes to die.
God, what's the point of trying.
I overwhelm myself with all of this potential, single words written on my limbs in the middle of the night to remind myself of an idea that will never be something tangible to grasp and hold onto. Bask in its awe of 'wow, I created that.'
I can't create everything. That's the worst part of it.
My thoughts, stay my thoughts.
As time slips away.
There will never be another me, another one to make what I long so desperately to.
An abyss somewhere of all the scrapped movie scenes, ruined art projects, or poems no one ever got to write.
I'm here, I'm real, and willing, I'll fight for my right to write, into the night, no holding back, no

backing down until I'm found, finding myself in
the lines and words my own hands make, don't
you dare try taking that away from me.
That's your mistake.
I'm not letting myself make the mistake of not
making, because of how drained I am at the end
of each day, sinking into my bed, with nothing
but dread of how empty I feel from being so full
of thoughts that won't escape.
Please free me, my art, from this overwhelming,
shrouding abyss
Of everything I wanted to come into this world
that couldn't escape.
Let me make my mark on this world-
Not a scratch but an indent, a deep scrape,
Simply using everything, I will create.
If only I had time,
Who has time to be creative anymore?
I do. I'll make some.
Just how I'll make myself into the artist I long to
become.
The problem with art is that someday you have
to stop making it.
Someday I will draw my last drawing.
Write my last poem.
Doodle my last doodle.
Someday, every idea I've had, noted down in the
margins of books or in between my test answers,

since I realized I could write, will never be anything more than forgotten, or misunderstood.
When you start creating, and truly noticing what is worthy of art- the world lights up with ideas that start pouring, flooding your mind faster then you know how to contain them.
Some stay as great ideas with awful execution, some never turn to anything more at all.
A forgotten graveyard of ideas in the middle of the night I never happen to remember.
Once you realize your potential, death, which is inevitable, becomes completely unbearable.
How much more could I have created if I had just lived another day? Year? 5? 10? 100?
I could create every hour I'm alive from now until I exhale for the final time. I've debated attempting it before.
Could I ever possibly refine and bring every single one of my mere thoughts into existence?
When I'm gone, most will barely look at what I've already created, let alone what I could have contributed to my world.
The real question is, how much would it have mattered at all…?
Not unless I've made my true mark in this world.
So let me. Please.
Let me Make my Mark.

Poetry Hurts

Poetry hurts.
As I find the words that express the deepest parts
of myself-
My soul finds a home, I feel seen-
How painful is it to stare into your own self in
its deepest form.
How painful is it to find the truth, and face it
dead in the eyes.
Poetry I find is a lost treasure, archives of
emotions we all feel,
Yet only some have found how to express.
It's incredible how connected to a strangers
words I can feel,
Maybe this is our way of connecting that piece
of stardust in each of us,
that somehow connects our souls.

We're not so different. All of us.
Poetry, art, and music have proved that, I think.
All the lonely poets, writing poems in solitude-
May I befriend you all?
Can we write poems together?
It's funny how we are all together in our
Solitude and loneliness.
We're all lonely at the same time-

Feeling the same sadness.
I guess art is our way to connect and express
Whatever stardust it is we were all made from.

I am incapable of anything
But admiration.
How far will admiration
take me in this life?

I think I need to romanticize my life to prove I
am worth anything at all.
What is the point to my suffering if there is
nobody sympathizing with me right now?
What is the point to my crying alone in my room
if this will not be a movie scene one day?
What will this loneliness achieve if no one ever
sees it?

I ask rhetorical questions a lot in my work,
Ones I know will never have an answer.
I don't write them in search of a solution,
I write them to find others with the same
questions,
And grow a bit closer to the truth.

This world is too beautiful to grasp and
comprehend.
Tears are pending, constantly
As I witness every crevice

Of what could be considered art around me.
A plastic bag, carried by the wind.
A book waiting to be read.
The way water rolls off my skin.
Someone's faded tattoo, or scar.
The flow of the knots in my door.
Every small fiber of my favorite pillow.
A song so perfectly made, it fills me to the brim
of feelings I can't hold.
Let them fall. Let them drip.
Let them roll down my cheeks and back into this
earth,
That has caused me so much-
So much.

You said I was being dramatic in my poetry.
Searching for attention.
What else is poetry if not dramatized, artistic
emotions?
What else is teenage angst if not poetry?
I'm still alive, and I would like to give myself
the space to be dramatic in my words.
I will share these poems until I cannot feel.
The few people who see them, thank you.
The fewer people who read and gain from them-
Please keep writing and feeling and being
dramatic.
Life is too beautiful and vast to be dull towards
it.

Here's my tiny perspective, my microscopic
contribution, my words I write in the late nights
and early mornings to make this life bearable
and process the fact of existence.
Let me overdramatize a bit.

I want to kiss you,
I want to love you,
I want to forget you.
I want to do everything I did,
And never did,
And wanted to do,
And wish I did.
With you.
I want lay on our backs,
Painful,
In a secluded field
As the rain hits our faces and ruins our clothes.
Let me feel, let me live,
Slap me, kick me, scratch me out of this.
Kill me, something big, something awful,
something amazing-
Everything. Everything and a little bit more.
Something to focus on, to channel this energy
through,
A scream that lets my lungs explode and rattles
every rib.
Because this is too much for my body to handle.
I don't know where to put it all.

Dear Past

My 18th century friends,
I hope to live up to a fraction of your worth.
I am a poet myself, you know.
Not as poetic, (yet,) I fear.
I wish to lead a life of suicide and wild nights,
Writing my rebellious thoughts,
and feeling deeply beyond fame.
I hope I'm a poet in your eyes.
And I hope death is treating you well.

New poets, new books of poetry await me.
I wonder what they would think of my
Mediocore teenage writings.
I wonder what they would write about today.
I hope to read in wonder and awe,
At the writers before me.
And carve my own legacy with them someday.

I can't see myself in the future.
I don't know who I'll be.
I didn't think I'd live this long.
What will become of me?

Will I die, like I imagine,
Or will I live a greater life?

All I know is options tire,
I only wish to end this strife.

If I should die, just in my sleep,
That is alright with me.
I pray the lord my soul to keep,
If not then leave me be

I feel like a misunderstood art piece.
Nobody can understand what I am.
Or maybe I don't mean anything at all.

Maybe I can never be heard or understood in this
lifetime.
Maybe I have to die and let a teenager years
from now discover my words,
And fall in love with who I was.

Dear young poets, hundreds of years from now.
I hope the grass is still as green, and you may
still see the sun.
I wish I could ease your fears, and tell you what
death is like.
But alas, at my current breathing state I cannot
foresee.
I don't know if anyone will read this,
I hope they will someday.
And some lonely teenager will discover my
words,

Attribute them to their own life,
And begin writing.
And keep writing.
And let themselves create simply for the sake of
creating,
Until they are discovered.
I would read your work, dear poet.
If it comes from the soul, I say it's wonderful.
Keep writing wonderfully.

Remember,
Permanence is Temporary.

Fixed

My black nails are chipped.
I can fix them tomorrow,
I said yesterday.

Your eyes are mirrors.
Warped, exaggerated,
Giving me false hope.

Do you remember?
When my skin touched yours in awe?
Were you even there?

Well, I remember.
And I deeply miss it.
Indescribably.

I know I shouldn't,
But I imagine sometimes
That you never left

Your eyes are still true,
Your smile is still genuine,
And my nails are black

Love Letter to a Life of Lies

I want to feel something. Anything.
How angsty of me.
As my emotions swirl above my head and
always end in crying,
I'm done.
Give me something direct, something I can wrap
my hands around, squeeze and say 'This. This is
how I feel.'

Gosh that sounds nice.
Curse my ever-overwhelmed brain.

I think sometimes we all pretend we don't know
any better.
As we get older- we learn.
Some truths- suck.
I know better, at 18.
Some might say I'm just stupid, immature, and
aren't thinking things through.
But oh, I'm thinking all right.
I want a time before my taxes are due, to be
rebellious.
Pretend I don't know better.
Live risky, be bold, do things I'll regret while I
can.
A love letter of lies to my angsty teenage life.

Blame it all on hormones and underdeveloped
brains.
That sounds perfect to me.
I can't wait to look back and regret my teenage
years.

The time will pass anyway.
Every blink, a second on the clock dies,
Passes away, no longer exists,
Time will move forward
Whatever I do with this time,
It will pass.
It will pass away
It will pass anyway,
It will slip through my fingers, or feel like 12
years.
Whether I am kissing my best friend,
Or staring at my ceiling,
Eating or starving,
Existing or
Dead.
But I'm here. And the time will pass.

What matters now is all that matters,
As my existence is obsolete.
But I am apart of a bigger picture,
A powerful play,
A beautiful orchestra
That we call life.

Rotting to Rest

A forgotten piece of food rotting in the back of
the throat,
inside a pile of bones, long left vacant of a soul.
As fungus feeds and maggots squirm,
ripping apart the decomposing flesh,
Leaving behind burrowed holes in the skin,
A sign of their territorial presence.
This is no longer a human body, it is Sin City for
parasites.
It is a decaying breeding, gambling ground
for the creatures who feed on the dead.
I pray my someday corroding crust of a once
working body,
Will dissolve into the earth, allowing new souls
to blossom from me.
I pray no one will remember my face,
As the beeltes who never knew me, peel my skin
for their nests.
And all that was, and ever could have been, my
life,
Is finally at rest.

Plane Simple

The plane ascends into the stars,
As I gaze at the world below with all its specks
of light.
Our cute little habits, lighting up our favorite
areas when the sun waves goodnight.
The life that felt so big while I was in the middle
of it,
Those blinding lights on the ground,
Turning to immeasurable dots from the sky.

I take so many pictures
But why?
Pictures from a plane
I think my memory is so awful now,
I need photos to help me know who I am, and
what I've done.
How sad is that. How awful.

Things are never as pretty in pictures
The clouds are gorgeous tonight. The moon is
too.
I wish you could see it, I wish I could show you
but you'll just have to take my word for it.
I tried to take a picture but it couldn't capture the
glow of the moon in the way my eyes see it,

the surrounding hum of the plane,
the feeling of my brother asleep next to me,
the music playing in my ears,
or the way my hair feels resting on my
shoulders.
I'd show you a picture, but all you'll get is a
blurry dot I'll tell you is the moon.
When I could write you a poem filled with this
moment instead.

I have the most poetic epiphanies on planes.
Whether it's the movie I happened to watch, the
confined space where my thoughts run, the small
break from the earth, or watching human habits
miles above them.
The most frustrating thing about planes is I am
stuck in my looping thoughts. I cannot rush this
flight,
I cannot do anything by simply looking down on
the world I want to change.
There's a philosophical religious metaphor
somewhere in there pertaining to God and his
view of us.
But regardless.
Maybe it's a little nice to have a reason to force
myself to do nothing but spin in my own
thoughts.

No Instagram to scroll through, or friends to talk
to.
Just me and my wishes to change the world.
As soon as I get down there, I promise. I'll make
my life better.
But for now I'm stuck in the sky.
This beautiful, peaceful sky, and I am thinking
and tired.

I'm stuck on this song just as I am stuck in the
air.
Repetition is comfort.
Limitation is comfort.
Familiarity is comfort.
Maybe I'm done with comfort,
But it's all I have to offer myself right now.
I can't change the world inside the melody of
this song,
Or miles above the rest of my life.
Just wait, I'll be back soon,
And force myself into uncomfort for the sake of
change.

As the plane ascends into the clouds I once
believed were cotton candy,
I am hit with a wave of emotion too grand to fit
into a single song.
There are too many words inside me I'm not
sure how to say-

How do I justify my tears through listening to
the same melody on repeat until I let it wrap its
arms around me and become comfortable in this
lonely nostalgia.
I could write a poem about this.
But I think the fact I am floating through the
clouds I once believed were cotton candy is
enough.

There is more darkness than light, a natural state
of the world is peace.
The life I find myself so overwhelmed by slowly
gets smaller and smaller as I get further and
further away from it.
And suddenly I am no longer apart of this earth,
but miles above it.
That is where I find peace.
Where the specks are simply specks,
And I am simply me.

Weeping Bride

Fidgeting with a necklace.
What a girl thing to do,
Finding solitude in the soft metal that hangs
around her neck,
Meaning or not, the coldness is comforting.
The beads twisting around the chain,
As she pulls further into herself.
Her hands smell metallic now.
Is she still worthy of love in her anxious habits?
A self-loathing bride
Shattering glasses of former wine
Against her bare skin,
Creating new scars.
Her blood seeps through the lace
Like stars, in a black pool of a sky,
A pool she dips the edge of her dress in,
Staining it, darker than before,
Beads rolling off the silk as she smiles
Through wiping tears off her cheeks,
She dives.
Her veil, like a whale trailing behind her,
A sharks fin in the water,
Soaked and ruined.
Her hair dripping, fraying, splitting
She smiles as her mascara runs

Black long branches of sorrow and ecstasy
Follow the curves of her face.
The curves of her body ever so defined,
Outlining, clinging to her breasts,
The dress is valueless now.
She grins.
She is alone and admires her own beauty.
After all that's all that really matters.
Maybe she isn't so self loathing,
After ruining what she thought
Made her beautiful.

Forgetful Dreams

As often as I've said
'Let's forget this, move on, and deal with it
tomorrow.'
I've run out of opportunities to say that about.
There can be no more forgetting,
If there's nothing more to remember.
I've tried my hardest to forget every bit about
you,
Distract myself with food and friends.
But every night when my eyes drift close, and
dreams come to visit me.
Your eyes open again to meet mine.
Exactly as I remember them.
Maybe I can't forget after all.
How torturous.

At first I'd say I hope you forget all about us.
Because you don't deserve to remember the
good times,
When you were the cause of every bad time.

But honestly I think the most pain is stored in
remembering.
I hope you wake up at night and can't help but
remember.

How you hurt me,
Every painful joyous memory
 you chose to never go back to.
You too.
I hope you remember this too.

I never wanted anything temporary.
Who ever does.
But here we are.
Looking for some next "permanent" thing.
Or maybe permanence no longer exists.

All our late night plans, crying, talking, the
world, religion, life-
Suddenly over, in a single night.
Trapped forever in my memories, and scattered
poems.
Nothing more.
No, nothing more.

I miss who you were.
Almost as much as I miss who I was.
I know change is for the better.
But part of me is still mourning the innocent
kids we were-
Before we got to say goodbye to them.
And us.
And everything that was.
That will never be again.

Sticked to Death

Sticked to death.

Once you place a sticker-
It's permanent.
It's stuck, it's beautiful,
And trying to peel it back up to replace it is
much too risky so-
It's permanent.

And my anxiety cannot handle that kind of
responsibility or pressure.

When there's a sticker I love- I put it in a
drawer, and wait.
Until the perfect time, place, weather, feeling to
actually use it.
Usually that never comes.
And it sits, un-sticked in the drawer.

Life's too damn short to waste perfectly good
stickers.

When I die and meet an artless end,
All of those favorite, perfectly good stickers will
go to waste.

When I finally hold my breath and place them-
They become stuck and unusable.
Serving a purpose- but the anticipation of
potential possibilities is over.
It's there now.

As it slowly peels, losing its color and stick as
the days go by.
Until it is no longer permanent, and there is a
place for something new.

Sand castles are temporay and disappear with
each tide.
Who knows if the sand will ever remember its
shape.
Until a new child comes along to create one of
their own.

Tattoos are only permanent for a lifetime,
Until your flesh rots and the ink seeps into the
wood frame of your coffin.
And the art itself has met its funeral past your
own.

I love it.
The idea of
Letting art be, and pass,
And die.

Maybe there is artistry in death.
Or maybe that is too rebellious to say.

Little Friend

How demented is the boy
Who cradles the corpse
Of a little bird,
Recently deceased.
A day ago, he nursed it.
And here it is, returned.
Tell me, little boy.
Do you know what you now hold?
You released it.
It flew.
And here it has come, back to you.
In a different form.
Void of a soul.
It's not just sleeping, child.
It's gone.

Yet here you are.
You discovered it.
Laying on the porch.
As you hold and cradle it.
I can't tell,
Do you know?

You smile, a crooked smile, with tears in your
little eyes.

'He flew back to see me. My friend came back-
to see me again'
Oh child, how can I tell you the truth?
'That- that- makes my heart happy.'
Some small tears trickle down.
'Sleep well, little friend.'

You gently place the little corpse down.
Leaving it, at peace in the grass.
We walk back inside together, as your silent
tears fall.

I look back at your little friend.
I know it's dead.
But I can't help but wonder-
If it did come back to visit you.
In its dying days.
If it loved you like a friend too.
How silly to wonder if a bird could think that
complex.
It doesn't matter anymore what the bird once
thought.
It only made your heart happy.

It made you happy that it came to visit.
And maybe some happiness in finding peace,
It's no longer suffering, sweetheart.
It's now at rest. In your arms.
You once cradled a soul,

Then an empty body.
Now it is held once more by the earth.

Such a small friend, caused your smiles and
tears.
I hear the flap of birds wings, and twittering in
the trees as I gaze.
Birds fly by without a second thought.
But that one meant so much to you.
Thank you for loving it more than anyone did.
You'll see him again, love.
Someday, I promise.

You'll see your little friend once more.

Cherry Blood

My eyes don't fit quite right in their sockets.
I fear they never were mine.
Fishnets cover my scars,
As blood drips down my thighs.
I suck on cherry candy to feel some form of
pretty,
I never could stand lip gloss.
Tissues full of makeup, tears, and blood stains.
Thank you for holding them all.
I don't have anyone to cry with,
In the early insomniac am's.
My pillow will have to do I guess,
As I hum to myself through sobs.
Did I mention I sleep on the wrong side of the
bed?
I leave the window open when its raining,
And pray the lighting kills me.
My hair is too long now,
I wish to shave it all.
But it covers my cheeks, I've always despised.
Now I don't have to cut them off.
My disgusting breasts sneak through the collar
of my shirt.
My father wakes me up, I never want to leave
my dreams.

My laundry is wrinkled and hasn't been cleaned.
If I think I'll sleep through tomorrow, why
should I even bother?
I write poems in messages I never send,
And keep the memories I've ripped in
shoeboxes.
Fraying paper ends, and leaking markers against
the cardboard walls.
I used a permanent marker on my soul, and I
can't erase it anymore.
I just embrace the pain my body gives me.
Deafening cramps and back aches,
And fall asleep to imaginary voices.
No one is there to say I'll be ok.
Besides the voices in my head,
And Gods.

Mo(u)rning

I mourn everything that passes.
Every sign of change,
Is bittersweet.
When they stop selling your favorite childhood
snack in stores.
Of course you haven't gotten it in years.
But now even if you wanted to,
It's gone.
Falling asleep early,
Lights on,
Blankets off,
Baggy eyes,
Strange dreams.
Both a gift and a curse.
Like being carried from the car to your room,
Except no one is there to make sure you're not
too cold,
You're tucked in just right,
To check in if you've had a bad dream,
Or to turn out the light.

And you wonder why you feel attached to the
small things that leave.
When the toaster you've used every morning for
the past few years finally gives out.

When your old toothbrush becomes too frayed to
be used.
When you outgrow your favorite shirt.
Or lose a toy you never found again.
Now you're 18. And none of that matters.
But you still wish you got to say goodbye.

I already miss this moment.
By this time next year, all of our lives will be
spent apart more than together.
Only next month you'll be in different states,
different schools, only talking through our
middle-school group chat.
I will have had surgery and either lived or died.
You may all fall in love or find new friends,
people, jobs- move on with your lives.
Our teenage years are closer to their end than
their beginning. How odd is that-
I still remember your rosy-cheeked childhood,
sitting in wood chips on the playground, and the
first sleepovers we ever had.
Now this may be one of the last where anything
remains quite like this.
I hope you know I love you all.
In all of our new friends, romantic endeavors,
drama, pranks, we've stayed together, having
sleepovers where safety and fun are the
priorities.

It's only hitting me now, surrounded by your
oblivious sleeping selves how much I'm going
to miss this group.
The solidarity of having you all since we were
so young, to come to with all we needed.
God, I hope we never die.
You are friends I'm learning to cherish now
more than ever.
Now that this is coming to an end, and we're all
moving on to new chapters.
Please let's stay friends, stay connected, see
fireworks together every 4th of July, have
sleepovers again in the future with new stories to
tell.
I miss my high school days and summer
sleepovers while I am in the middle of one.
I know the time will fly,
And soon enough we'll be bridesmaids at each
others weddings,
Remembering the times when we all talked until
2 am and slept over.
Just like this.

I hope we're best friends. BFF's forever- but- for
real, not the 5th grade kind.
When you make eachother friendship bracelets,
and come to eachothers birthday parties-
Promising to be 'best friends forever.'

But life hits, one of you starts vaping and the
other turns out to be a lesbian and you fall apart.
You see eachother in the hallways, or eachothers
instagram posts,
Knowing you once promised to be 'best friends
forever,' but you changed.
And that's ok I guess-

I feel a 5th grade, trying to make that dumb
promise to myself again.
Can we really last forever this time?

Do you remember those innocent loves?
Before we knew the world?
Your sweet, tiny cheeks turning red as you see
your favorite person walk through the halls.
You smile and wave, praying for them to catch a
glance.
That fateful prince, how mature you thought he
was.
6 and a half, how out of your league, only half a
year older than you.
You try to sit by him in class, maybe share your
pencil with him, and feel some innocent
butterflies from the exchange.
"I'm in love," You thought to yourself.
You didn't even know what love is, some might
say.
But I'd disagree.

Maybe you once knew what the heart of love
was supposed to be.
You didn't know the impurities of the world.
When I was a little lovesick kid, I thought a kiss
on the lips was genuinely the pinnacle of human
existence.
That once I finally had my first true kiss, my life
would be complete.
I think I misunderstood what a kiss was.
In my 7 year old head,
'kiss' and 'cure' were synonyms.
Before you were hurt, before you realized there
were more feelings than butterflies, before you
knew all of the imperfections, the hurt, the
hardships, expectations, wants and needs of life.
But in that moment, all that mattered was that he
smiled when you gave him your pencil. You
would share answers and laugh together. And
you thought you were in love.
Maybe by now you've forgotten all about him.
Wondering where he is now.
After all of the hurt and pain you're now all-too
familiar with.
Wishing you could go back to a pencil-sharing,
innocent butterflies kind of relationship.
Go back to the beginning of learning what love
is.
I don't recognize myself now, after all the hurt.

Who is that little kid with bags under her eyes
and a sadness in her soul?
Only I know the tears that formed minutes after
the picture was taken.
But don't I look cute? My smiling face, my
hoodies and haircut and blushing cheeks.
You write so many letters to me but I am unable
to return the favor and tell you it will all be ok.
Oh innocent me in these pictures, you have no
idea what lies ahead. But you'll make it.
I promise you, you make it.
And learn to love yourself again.
Can I give you a hug? I know you need it. I
know… I know.
I miss her.
But I don't miss being her.
I wish the best for myself.
And that lonely little kid.

Although I am 18, I fear my independence
hasn't grown.
A five year old will insist on getting their own
water,
Then drop the cup, let the water spill,
And cry out of unmet expectations, and failures.
That's me.
I don't feel like me.

I am too pretty in those pictures.

I am too pretty in the mirror.
My hair falls perfectly today, more than
yesterday and there is no one to see it but me.
I see it. I appreciate it.
I love it. I want to be loved so bad- as I see love
in everything else, including pictures of me-
Oh don't you see?
You love yourself already.

I miss who you were.
Almost as much as I miss who I was.
I know change is for the better.
But part of me is still mourning the innocent
kids we were-
Before we got to say goodbye to them.
And us.
And everything that was.
That will never be again.

Conversational Poems

That's it, right? That's how this goes?
You give everything you are to someone,
Only for you to drift apart years later.
And you become something else,
And you give all you are again to someone else,
And the cycle repeats until you're not sure love
is real anymore.
And until you have enough breakup poems to
build a forest, and set it on fire.

You loved me then- why did I have to change?
We laughed, we talked,
Now there is empty space, and the air is full of
'could have beens'
I had to go and change, I had to be different.
I had to leave and experience life,
And now I am no longer loveable.
It's still in me somewhere- the parts you said
you loved.

I'm sorry I had to change.
I think it's still in me somewhere-
The parts you said you loved.
I know it's different now,
The air is heavy with silences,

I'm searching for the person you once liked,
I don't know if they exist anymore.
But I'm here…
Is that enough this time?
Or do you want the innocent me,
Before I hated and loved this much?

I know I ask too much, I send too much,
I never shut up, I'm always talking and wishing
and hoping and feeling-
I'm sorry.
I care absolutely, there is no other way.
Do you as well?
Or are we no longer the people we wanted each
other to be.

Is it all in my head? How wonderful you were?
If so, it's all in your head too.
I destroyed every piece of myself for you and
waited impatiently.
How wonderful for you.
You gave me a connection I continue to dream
of-
As it fades, I'm unsure if it was ever real.
But you're real again, in my life.
I don't think I know how to talk to you anymore,
Who's fault is that?

Don't you understand the yearning and poetry
that lies behind my eyes?
The avalanche of words I'm holding back,
because if I didn't I'd never stop?
What lies behind your eyes?
I can't see them, but I know they aren't hollow.
They're windows.
Please let me see… open the curtains a little bit
more.
I'll open mine too.

I love too much, I love too deeply.
It seeps past my bones and into the very essence
of my existence.
I cannot love in shallow waters,
I'll offer my hand from the depths of sea
And pray you care to join me.
Or at least swim a little further from the shore.
I'll meet you there. I promise.

Maybe in another life.
What a nice thought, but what a lie it is.
There is no other life. There is only this one.
There is only this moment, this time and place-
this day.
This is the life I have with or without you.
These are where our experiences lie.
Please god, let it be this life.

Let me live in my delusions.
No I won't be meeting you at an airport and
falling in love,
No I won't go to your college Halloween party
hours away,
No I won't win so many awards or publish a
poetry book this year,
No we can't be friends the same way we were
before,
No I know there is no other life other than this
one,
I know.
But let me pretend, for a moment,
For a night,
It's all true.

Do you know how much I write about you? And
how much I want to?

Everything I want to say about you
Cannot be said in a single poem.
A collection, a poetry book,
Or an entire filled library.
Maybe our conversations are a poem in
themselves.
Maybe the very fact we found each other is a
poem that cannot be captured in words. Maybe
not everything can be confined to a form of art-
When it, itself is a form of art already.

Who Else But Everyone?

I dream of love and death,
Hand in hand together, often.
I dreamt of you again,
I thought I was done with that.
But I do miss your hand, your hugs,
Having your shoulder to lean and cry on.
I wake up and you're gone,
I wonder if I should tell you.
But I don't.
I get up, eat some food, and move on.
While memories of your love flashes in my
mind.

I miss knowing you would be there.
Even if you weren't really there,
I got to imagine you were.
And know that you would be.

Now, I don't know if you would be.
So who is there left to imagine?

Who else can handle me like this?
And if I can handle myself- what was the point
of all that?

"I remembered what you told me- this was your
favorite thing."
"Oh. Yeah that used to be my favorite, but things
change."
Why do even favorites change?
I used to know what you liked-
I loved the things you liked for you-
And now…
I used to be your favorite too.
But things change.

There are too many things I cannot tell a soul,
Besides one day the closest person to me.
But by then I will have forgotten half my stories,
And someday they will leave and forget them
too.
And I'll have more memories I'll soon never
remember,
And more experiences I cannot tell a soul.

I'm perfectly content with being single until I
need a hug.
My period of pain and suicide always called for
me to need someone else.
Any physical body to lean on and find comfort
in,
A body that is not my own. Please.
Can I lean on you in the back of the car? Can we
pretend we are lovers for a moment?

I'll be me again soon, I promise.

The scenarios I create of you in my head,
Are more real than the atoms of your hands.
I'll dream you are here, while I haven't seen
your face,
I'll remember you like a summer day,
And let you go all the same.

May the Fourth Be

May the fourth
Be in your memories.

We roam the cloudy gray skies,
A girl, a boy, and I.
After a long day of Act 1, Abba songs,
Some ice cream and woodchips,
That will hold our emotions as they pass.

Dangling from plastic playgrounds,
Talking about love, life,
What kisses feel like.
What crushes feel like.
Awkward times to look away,
But awkward times to gaze.
My shoes, between the metal, smiling.

We stumble over the bridge, creaking as we go.
The stream trickling beneath our feet, its muddy
glory
As the sky sprinkles rain drops to the tops of our
heads.
Enough to make us blink and flinch,
And hold our hands out for more.

Nows the perfect time, perhaps,
For him to say he's scared of Thunder.
As the sky screams, roars and flashes,
Growing grayer as the snaps turn to stomps in
the sky-

Me and the girl laugh along the cracks in the
sidewalk,
As the worms emerge and our clothes grow
damp.
Our newly-ripped shirts, paralleled.
The impulsive thoughts must have reached us in
unison,
As we both had ripped the collars off our shirts
that morning.
Her fishnets, fraying at the knees, as water rolls
down her ankles.

From damp to soaked, as it pours on us,
Enclosing our tiny town,
Our broken bodies,
Our fragile friendships
In shattering patters of water
Hitting our skin and hair
As our clothes stick to us,
And the echoes of change reach our ears
We shriek in emotional joy.

We reach a field of new leaves and new mud,

Our new territory, shelter from society
To enjoy our joy in peace.
Basking in nature's blessing,
And eachother's comforting company.
Our bare feet in the grass, like children again.
We skip, frolic, run, scream, laugh hysterically,
jump to the heavens, we reach our hands up for
more.
Like a child begging her mother to be held.

I don't remember if I was crying.
It was probably just the rain.

"I wouldn't be mad if I died here."

Then let's die here. Let's forget the world,
Let our souls crumble into the soil of this
forgotten field,
Intertwining into oil as the years go by.
Zeus can strike us through our embrace.
Hands clasped, electricity pulsing through our
veins,
In one way or another, as we shook with our
final breath,
And were finally one with each other,
And God.

Gosh, let me die there in the memory.

But I can't. (Can I?)

Because as we lie side by side on our backs,
Water seeping down our cheeks with open arms,
I sit up and say-

"This is the kind of day I'm glad I'm still here
for."

We find our place,
As the patters grow softer and smaller.
Heavy, feels the air, although the clouds begin to
part.
It's vulnerable, having wet hair around people.
The self-consciousness of running makeup and
revealing shoulders creeps in.

The small budding flowers interject as we toss
them between each other.
Ripping them from their roots for our mere
entertainment,
They're beautiful in their dying. I hope I will be
too.
We lick the pesticides off blades of grass, as we
talk about French kissing.
We say things we wouldn't say anywhere else.
The field catches our secrets and holds them safe
and away from the world.

Love is a peculiar thing.

Spongy shoes, puddles of sludge. We make our
way back through the field.
A frog in our path, as we hold it, tease it, adore
it, and squeal.
Just my type, they joke.
Just my type.

I walk with them in the road, under a gentle pink
sky.
Squeaking shoes, shivering shoulders, fresh
mosquito bites.
Damp, stained denim and a ripped sweater
tucked into my bra strap.
We talk about death.
As we slap the leaves on the trees along our
path,
Giving us tiny shimmering reprises to our
rainstorm.

We reach the end of the sidewalk.
And wave goodbye.
Absent-minded smiles.
It's off to Mexico.
Oklahoma.
Anesthesia.

I walk home alone.

Gently touch the leaves on my walk.
Humming 'singing in the rain,'
Skipping and twirling along.
In my pink-skied ecstasy
Of knowing I lived.

Lonely Echo

When I'm alone,
And I mean really alone,

The kind of feeling that sinks deep into your
soul, letting you remember you have one.
When the room you've grown up in and the bed
you've slept in for years don't feel so familiar
anymore. And a strange part of you, is longing
for the feeling of home.
The same awareness when you're the first one
awake at a sleepover, early in the morning.
The homesickness that washes over you, waking
up in someone else's bed, alone, with your
friends dozing beside you, the emptiness of
being left alone with nothing but your own
existence.

It's the kind of loneliness that comes with
staying awake at 4 am,
looking at your own hands questioning if
they've ever really been yours.
Or why you're even alive to begin with.

An echoing silence, with buzzing thoughts,
hitting the walls of your room, mirroring the

impression of a damp, dripping cave. My silent
tears, mimicking the drizzle down my cave
walls.

Sometimes, when life feels that way I do this
silly, stupid thing.
I talk to the echo, praying it talks back.
'Sweetheart' I call myself. 'You'll be ok.'
I know the darkness can't do anything more than
consume my words.
But the echo is all that matters.
'Just take some deep breaths. This will pass.' my
echo coos to me.
I know who I imagine the echo to be.

My lonely cave of a room feels just that much
safer.
'You're not alone.' My echo tells me.
'Thank you.' I respond.

Wanting to Last Forever

Daylight Savings.
It's cute how we attempt to manipulate time,
Just to have another hour of precious light in the
day.
We remember to change our clocks,
Form new sleep schedules and habits,
Throw our bodies off course-
All for the sake of basking in the precious sun's
glow just a bit longer.
dreaming and longing for just a bit more time.
Isn't that what we all crave?
Just a little bit longer.
Just a minute more.
Two minutes more.
An hour.
A day.
Another lifetime.
Please just let me enjoy earth's beauty for as
long as humanly possible.
Just a little more than a lifetime longer.
When you realize all you want to do is live.
Death becomes your adversary instead of a
neutral acquaintance.
The realization you want to live will hit you, in
the middle of an incredible moment.

The kinds of moments you wish can last longer
than forever.
Until you realize they won't.
And suddenly you're on your knees, begging
God to eliminate death for this moment.
And the inevitability of non-existence is no
longer a neutral face in the distance,
But becomes a stealer of joy, with a wrinkled
face and an ominous gloom.
Looming over your every move.
And the life you finally want to live,
Begins a countdown, a ticking clock with a time
limit.
That is what wanting to live costs you.
You need to make the most of it,
Because no one lasts forever.
How tragic is it.
To only live once.
Only one lifetime to experience,
Everything only one lifetime can hold.
I can never have every relationship ever.
I can never possibly get to know everyone in the
closest ever ways.
I can never enjoy the foods I hate.
I can never write every poem,
Create every art piece,
See everything there ever is to see, even just this
year.
I can never relive my childhood,

I can never jump forward in time.
I can never be someone completely other than
who I am.
We're so limited to our experiences.
And our experiences are- abundant.
I'm overwhelmed on a daily basis just living as
an average person,
And yet it scares me how finite my existence is.
How inevitable death is as a concept.
It's there, I'm here.
And what's between is just a straight,
unwavering line until everything that could have
been,
Can never be.

Letting the Ferris Wheel Turn

Life loves doing this, it loves changing
everything at the same time and letting
everything completely start over from scratch,
letting me take nothing with me but memories.

You have so many poems written about you, you
don't even know.
Ones I've never shared with you, but are right
there for you to see.
So many I wish you could read and understand
what I'm trying to tell you.
Writing you poetry is easier than talking to you.
I can say things like 'let's kiss on a Ferris wheel'
And you'd think 'What an interesting metaphor'
While I sit across from you with red lips on a
Ferris wheel.
Waiting patiently and learning to
Let go.
Of her, of you,
Of who I was and could have been,
Of past mistakes,
The color of my room I never changed,
My broken bike I never learned to ride.
The kiss we could have had, but the ride came to
an end,

And the next cart passed us by.
Goodbye,
Let me go.
What is this. What is this life.
Why does everything worth loving
Have to age, and fade.
Am I destined to miss all my memories and
search for you in everyone I meet?
Am I only here to say I was?
And nothing more…

Ya know that no ones perfect?
People are just- people?
And that's ok.
People are wonderful.

Life is just- life?

Wow. Life is just-
Life.

And that's wonderful too.

Don't Look at Me; Read Me

My most poetic time is when my hair finally
drys.
It brushes my shoulders now, too long, but soft.
When I watch the blood drip down the drain,
And the skin peel from my fingers.
The thunder outside reminds me of you,
And my insides ache for help.
There are tears pending behind my eyes,
My spine wants a place to rest,
But you haven't read my poems yet.
So I stay up and wait for you to.
Soon? Please say it's soon.
Praying no one hears
my gentle hums into the night
As I type away my little midnight metaphors.

Stay

Hi. I want to read a poem.
It's a poem I wrote. I wouldn't say it's great, or
even remotely worth the wait.
But then again my friends all say I
underestimate myself,
I guess this is the antidote for my
self-depreciation, my hesitation to begin this
poem is evidence of my anxiety as I stand upon
this stage, and pause, and wait, and hesitate
again as I repeat-
"I want to read a poem."
The poem I want to read is called 'Stay.'
It's about- procrastinating, awaiting the
fascinating phenomena of witnessing time
passing and overthinking your way through it,
attempting to calm your racing mind, lined with
anxiety-
With the goal of aspiring to stay in the okay
moments of life just a little bit longer.
I would begin this poem.
But by the time it begins, with each new word I
say since I stepped on this stage, I am creeping
closer to the end, closer to the applause, closer to
me stepping offstage, heading home, going to
sleep, going to school, graduating, getting a job,

getting a life soon enough I'm 40 years old,
some weird forgotten artist with 10 cats in a
small one room apartment wondering where did
this moment go?
It's here. It's right here.
Stay.
I'm afraid this poems already begun. I'm afraid
it's still going- soon enough, it will be done. In
the long run, I'm sure people will say this was
well-done but as I'm performing there's nothing
that can be un-done.
As anxious as I am about performing, I really
just want to stay here, and feel like I am here.
Why is that such a difficult request to make
true?
I write too much, I talk too much, I think too
much- I'm never just here enough.
I can never just be here- I need to be something
more.
I need to change the world- if I dont then what
am I here for??
I'm supposed to move on after this year, into
college and jobs and moving out and life-
Did you know it never ends?
Every day ends with the beginning of the next,
again, and again, and again, and again.
The summer used to feel like a break, but now
nothing feels like anything because this life is
just rolling downhill so freaking fast, I can't

catch up with it, and stumble as I try. Because I
not only need to catch up, I need to be ahead,
ahead of everything, ahead of it all, helping
others with theirs too, because what is my
purpose if I'm simply just here.
What is the point of this poem?
To show you my thoughts, how my mind can be.
And I bet a lot of your minds are in a similar
place right now.
Part of you is listening to what I'm saying, while
in the back of your mind you're thinking of how
you need to fold the laundry, and walk the dog,
and finish every dream you had when you were
in high school. Everything you need to get done
for this life, for this week, for tomorrow, for
tonight-
I wanted to write a poem that would resonate
with everyone. End in a big finale, make
everyone contemplate their life choices, and
graduate from this school with an epic mic drop.
But maybe it's ok to write something about
myself for once. Write about what I know.
To realize the only moment you have right now
is this one.
The moment I have your attention, and the
moment you're listening.
I long to hear the applause. I long to let myself
hear it. To bask in it, for once. I don't think I've
ever actually heard the applause given to me.

Today I'm going to try to stay.
No matter what is on your mind in this moment,
from the busiest to the calmest- I ask you leave
with one thing.
Stay in the moment once and awhile.
Slow down to smell the roses, stop to enjoy the
sun or rain or snow, pause to let yourself bask in
the words you are hearing or the art you are
experiencing. Take your time experiencing and
creating in this world.
Even if you have so much to do, even if you
dont feel like you deserve it- it's ok to just slow
down. To just breathe.
All we have is this one moment, and then it's
gone like an eyelash to the wind.
The days keep rolling, and this poem keeps
getting closer to the end, and the seconds keep
slipping away.
Just stay.
Please stay.
Stay here, stay in the moment, stay present, stay
alive, stay living.
And tomorrow will come a little slower.
And the moments will last a little longer.
Now the end of this poem is only five lines
away,
And with that I only have one thing left to say-
Carpe Diem. Seize the day.
Please make the most of your life.

And just-
Stay.

www.ingramcontent.com/pod-product-compliance
Lightning Source LLC
LaVergne TN
LVHW050928200726
843508LV00011B/2290